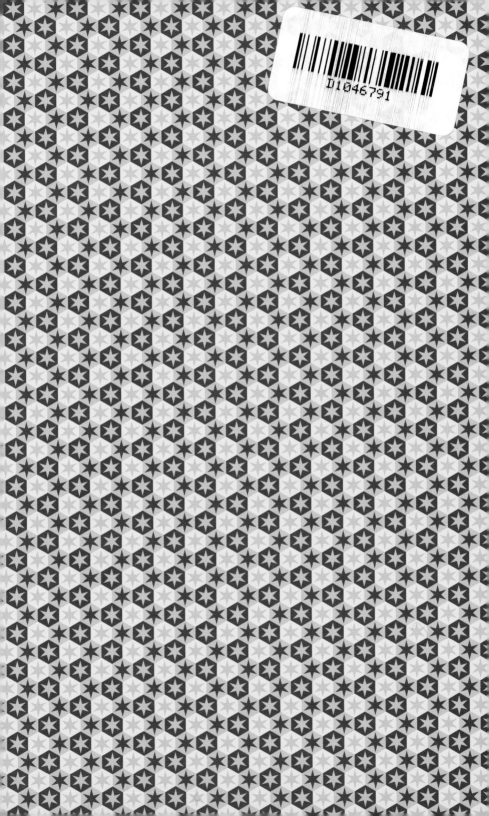

Wonders OF His Love

Finding Jesus in Isaiah

Champ Thornton

Illustrated by
Jeremy Slagle

Introduction

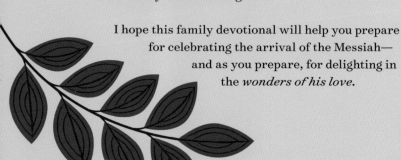

The word *advent* means arrival.
For kids it may mean the never-ending
weeks before the arrival of Christmas gifts.

But the season of Advent is when Christians remember
the long-awaited arrival of the Messiah. During these
weeks, as we look forward to Christmas, we stand
in the sandals of those who waited centuries for the
arrival of the One God had prophesied would come.

One of these prophets was Isaiah. His prophecy spans
66 chapters and contains over 37,000 words in English.
Isaiah uses some of his words to paint pictures—flocks
and fruit, roots and roads, swimmers and shepherds.
He helps us see the real-world connections between
God's truth and God's world.

Wonders of His Love: Finding Jesus in Isaiah will help
your family visualize the main portrait Isaiah paints—
of the promised and long-awaited Messiah.

In each week of this family devotional, there are five
short devotionals to read aloud. Each one is intended
for even little children to grasp. You'll also find fun
bonus sections, as well as crafts and activities to help
make family memories together.

I hope this family devotional will help you prepare
for celebrating the arrival of the Messiah—
and as you prepare, for delighting in
the *wonders of his love.*

Contents

Week One

The First Wonder

Jesus Is the Light of the World and He Makes Us See

Day 1: Picture It

Light Shines in the Darkness

The people who walked in darkness have seen a great light; those who dwelt in a land of deep darkness, on them has light shone. Isaiah 9:2

Have you ever tried to walk in the dark? Let's try something simpler. Close your eyes. No looking around.

Now without opening your eyes—try to touch your nose. Easy, right?

Close your eyes again. In your mind, pick out something in the room related to Christmas—a wreath, a stocking, an ornament. Try to point at it. Keep pointing. Open your eyes. Were you close?

Can you imagine living in the dark?
Always night, and never day?

Some animals love the dark.
They sleep during the day and play at night.

Bats and rats. Owls and aardvarks.
God made them able to see at night.

But how would you do in the dark? Could you find your toys? Your room? Your friends? Your nose?

We're not made for the dark. We need the light.

But for thousands of years, most people lived in darkness. Not in darkness of night but in darkness of heart. Ever since the first people sinned against God, they were born not being able to see what they were doing, and they couldn't see what God was doing.

They were in the dark. They thought they knew what God wanted. They thought they knew the right way to him. They thought if they could just worship the right God, it would be OK—so they worshiped hundreds of gods just to be safe.

They thought if they could just be good enough, it would be OK—so they tried to be perfect. And then sometimes (lots of times) they just gave up trying and did whatever they wanted.

But like walking in the dark, without God no one could find their way. And people ended up getting hurt. In the dark, they tripped on things and crashed into each other. Without God, they stumbled and fumbled along.

But the darkness wasn't around them, it was in them. They couldn't just turn on the light. They needed someone to open their eyes, to lead them from darkness to light.

And someone did.

God gave light to his people. Hundreds of years before Jesus was born, the prophet Isaiah announced what God was going to do about the darkness in people's hearts. He promised: "The people who walked in darkness have seen a great light; those who dwelt in a land of deep darkness, on them has light shone" (Isaiah 9:2). Jesus is the promised Light of the World.

Questions

What's so bad about living in the darkness of the heart?

Why is it so good that Jesus is the light of the world?

Day 2: A Closer Look

Jesus Is the Light

And in the same region there were shepherds out in the field, keeping watch over their flock by night. And an angel of the Lord appeared to them, and the glory of the Lord shone around them, and they were filled with great fear. And the angel said to them, "Fear not, for behold, I bring you good news of great joy that will be for all the people. For unto you is born this day in the city of David a Savior, who is Christ the Lord. And this will be a sign for you: you will find a baby wrapped in swaddling cloths and lying in a manger." And suddenly there was with the angel a multitude of the heavenly host praising God and saying, "Glory to God in the highest, and on earth peace among those with whom he is pleased!"

When the angels went away from them into heaven, the shepherds said to one another, "Let us go over to Bethlehem and see this thing that has happened, which the Lord has made known to us." And they went with haste and found Mary and Joseph, and the baby lying in a manger. Luke 2:8–16

On the night when Jesus was born, the nighttime sky shone like day—bursting with blazing light and angel song. A Savior had been born.

When the shepherds came to see Jesus, they stepped out of the dark streets into the light of that tiny room. And for the first time, they could see the Son—whose life would shine and whose death would bring the darkness to an end.

And when the child grew up, whatever he said and did were like rays of early morning sunlight piercing the night's darkness (John 1:5).

How did Jesus bring light to the world?

He took every dark thing and shone the light of his love on it. When he cleansed the lepers, you could see the light of his love. When he healed the sick, his light shone. When he raised the dead, light broke into the darkness. His light of love was the light of life (John 1:4).

Questions

What did Jesus do in the Bible that amazes you the most? Why?

What has Jesus done for you that amazes you the most? Why?

Day 3: A Promise to Remember

You Will Never Be Alone

I will turn the darkness before them into light, the rough places into level ground. These are the things I do, and I do not forsake them. Isaiah 42:16b

Are you sometimes worried that you are all alone?

It's true that wanting to go our own way and not God's way (what the Bible calls sin) has separated us from God (Isaiah 53:6). We are far from God, and we can't get back. We are lost in darkness. But Jesus can bring us back.

Jesus always walked in the light (John 8:12). He always went God's way (Philippians 2:8). He always loved God and loved people. He didn't fight with his brothers and sisters. He didn't make fun of anyone. He didn't disobey his parents.

So when he died on the cross, he didn't give his life for his own sins. He gave his life for ours (1 John 3:16). All we have to do is turn to him and ask for forgiveness and he will forgive and welcome us into his family. And he gives us new eyes to see God.

Now we can be sure that God will always be with us (Hebrews 13:5). We will never be forsaken. We will never be all alone. We can see clearly to follow Jesus. He is the light of the world.

Because of him, we will live in the light of God's love, not only at Christmas but every day of every year.

Questions

What would heaven be like if Jesus weren't there?

Would you still want to go if Jesus wouldn't be there?

Day 4: A Challenge to Accept

We Are the Light of the World

"You are the light of the world. A city set on a hill cannot be hidden." Matthew 5:14

Here's something amazing. Not only does Jesus say he is the light of the world but then he turns right around and says to his followers, "You are the light of the world" (Matthew 5:14). How can that be? It turns out that when we ask Jesus for forgiveness and put our faith in him, then he lives in us and his light shines through us.

Jesus gives us the job of shining the light of his love on the world around us (Matthew 5:14). Just like you can see the lights of a city from far away, so you can see, from a long ways away, the light of God's love shining in the kind things Christians do for others.

Do you know anyone you can shine the love of Jesus on today? What about someone at school—someone the other kids aren't very nice to? What about a neighbor? What about your brothers and sisters? It can be especially hard to love your own family!

Did you know that sometimes people get extra sad at Christmas time? They miss their families or they see others getting gifts and their own families don't have enough money for gifts. Is there someone your family could share God's love with this Christmas? Think about that together.

Maybe you can start a new tradition of shining the love of Christ on someone or some family at Christmas time every year. Jesus is the light of the world, and when you help others, his light shines through you.

Questions

How can you shine your light this week?

Who are some people that you could help or encourage?

Day 5: Family Fun

There is another way that light was used to announce the birth of Jesus, the Light of the World. In Matthew 2:1–11, read the story of the wisemen who, following the bright light of the "star," found Jesus, the light of the world.

After this Christmas carol, you'll find lots of fun for the whole family: crafts and other activities.

O Come All Ye Faithful

O come, all ye faithful,
joyful and triumphant,
O come ye, O come ye to Bethlehem.
Come and behold him,
born the king of angels.

Refrain:
O come let us adore him,
O come let us adore him,
O come let us adore him,
Christ the Lord.

Sing, choirs of angels,
sing in exultation,
sing, all ye citizens of heav'n above:
"Glory to God,
all glory in the highest!" [Refrain]

Yea, Lord, we greet thee,
born this happy morning,
Jesus, to thee be all glory giv'n;
Word of the Father,
Late in flesh appearing. [Refrain]

Craft

Week 1: Ornament

Supplies You'll Need: Week 1 ornament craft (one copy for each child); coloring/art supplies; scissors; glue stick or tape; yarn or string. Note: Scan the QR code at the back of the book to access digital copies of the ornament crafts.

Directions: Cut out the ornament copy and have the children decorate the design. Read the "Isaiah says" and the "Jesus says" statements. Then have the children write their answer to the "I say" statement. Fold the ornament on the dotted line. Make a string or yarn loop for hanging and tuck it into the fold. Tape or glue the ornament closed.

Ornament Questions

What does Isaiah say?
Answer: "A light will shine."

What does Jesus say?
Answer: "I am the light."

What do we say and believe?
Answer: "Jesus makes me see."

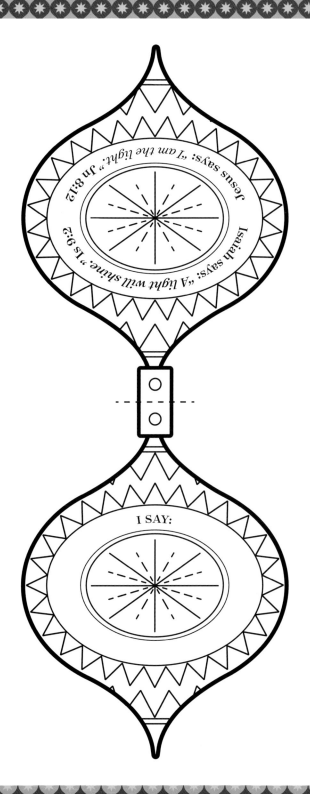

Jesus says: "I am the light." Jn 8:12

Isaiah says: "A light will shine." Is 9:2

I SAY:

Other Activities

All of this week's activities involve light (e.g., stars, glow sticks, flashlights). In each one you'll have an opportunity to discuss how Jesus is the light of the world and makes us see.

Activity #1

Use this recipe, or one of your choice, to make Christmas cookies in the shape of stars. After the cookies are cooled, frost/decorate them.

Sugar Cookie Stars

Yield: 5 dozen

Ingredients:
1 ½ cups unsalted butter, softened
2 cups white sugar
4 eggs
1 teaspoon vanilla extract
5 cups all-purpose flour
2 teaspoons baking powder
1 teaspoon salt

Directions

1. In a large bowl, beat together butter and sugar until smooth and creamy. Beat in eggs and vanilla. Stir in the flour, baking powder, and salt until combined well.

2. Divide the dough in half and shape each half into a ball. Wrap the balls separately in plastic wrap and chill for at least one hour.

3. Preheat oven to 400 degrees F. On a floured surface, roll out the dough, one ball at a time, ⅛- to ¼-in. thick. Cut into shapes with a star-shaped cookie cutter. Place cookies 1 inch apart on ungreased cookie sheets.

4. Bake 6 to 8 minutes in preheated oven. Cool completely.

Activity #2

Supplies You'll Need: flexible glow sticks

Glow Stick Ring Toss

Bend flexible glow sticks, which you can get at most stores, into circles. Then turn out the lights and play a "ring toss" game. Each person gets three chances to toss their glow-stick circle onto a door knob. (Or you could play tic-tac-toe using glow stick circles as "Os" and glow sticks taped into "Xs".)

Activity #3

Supplies You'll Need: pen; paper; flashlight; small prize

Scavenger Hunt

Create a scavenger hunt, by writing short descriptions on pieces of paper and hiding them around your home (examples below). Then with everyone holding or sharing a flashlight, turn off the lights, and go from one clue to the next, letting your children guess where the next clue might be. You can have a special prize (like candy or a small gift or surprise) waiting at the end of the hunt.

Clue Examples:

1 Start with this clue: I'm the first clue, and I'm hiding in a place that's dark and cold.

2 In the refrigerator/freezer: I'm the next clue, but I'm working under cover.

3 In someone's bed: I'm the next clue, and I want to star in my own show.

4 Near the television: I'm the final clue, and I have a gift for you.

5 The final clue is under the Christmas tree or in a Christmas stocking.

Was Jesus Born in a Stable?

And she gave birth to her firstborn son and wrapped him in swaddling cloths and laid him in a manger, because there was no place for them in the inn.
Luke 2:7

You might think Jesus was born in a stable because Luke 2:7 says baby Jesus was laid in a manger—a feeding trough for animals. People throughout church history have offered reasons why Jesus might have been born in a barn-like shed, an open-air barnyard, a cave, or even in a shepherd's tower.

But none of these suggestions quite work. First, no one in Jesus's world would have turned away even an unexpected guest (Luke 11:6). The word "inn," really means "guest room" (Luke 22:11). There was no space for them in a guest room.

Joseph and Mary didn't get turned away from the Bethlehem Hotel at the last minute. In fact, they hadn't arrived at the last minute at all. Luke says, "And while they were there, the time came for her to give birth" (Luke 2:6). "While they were there"—not, "just as they skidded into town, barely making it in time!"

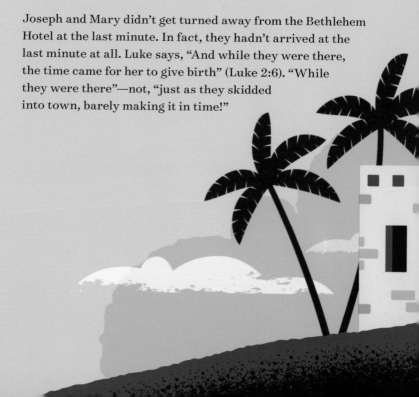

It seems that Joseph and Mary arrived in plenty of time. But the guest room was already occupied by others. So, where does that leave us? More to the point, where does that leave Joseph and Mary?

Ancient houses were sometimes split-levels, with an upper living area and attached guest room and a lower area to lodge animals at night (1 Samuel 28:24). (Even today, residents in rural areas of Switzerland for example, often house animals on the lower level of their homes—providing security for livestock and some additional warmth to the house.) And in this kind of house, mangers were often little holes carved into the edge of the floor right before it dropped off to the lower level.[1]

So even if Jesus wasn't born in a cave or a barn, he was born in a humble place. He's a Savior for men, women, and children from all levels of society. And that is indeed "good news of great joy that will be for all the people" (Luke 2:10).

Week Two

The Second Wonder

Jesus Is the Fruitful Branch
and He Gives Us Life

Day 1: Picture It

We Need God's Life

*Out of the stump of David's family will grow a shoot—
yes, a new Branch bearing fruit from the old root.
And the Spirit of the LORD will rest on him—the Spirit
of wisdom and understanding. Isaiah 11:1–2a NLT*

What kind of Christmas tree do you like best?

Do you like trees filled with decorations? Some trees are stiff
and prickly but can hold lots of ornaments.

Or do you prefer trees with a perfect triangle shape? Or
perhaps your favorite trees fill the house with a wonderful
smell all through the Christmas season.

(Or maybe any tree will do—as long as it's surrounded by gifts
and presents.)

But even the best Christmas trees don't last, do they? Unless
you have a fake tree, you have to give it water. If you don't, it'll
dry and shrivel up. Why? Because it's not connected to the
roots anymore. Without the roots, the tree is dead.

The roots provide everything the tree needs. The roots keep
the tree fresh and green and alive.

A long time ago, God's people thought they could live without
God—the God who provided everything they needed. But they
didn't obey him, love him, or trust him. They thought they
could live on their own (Ezekiel 34:6).

Before long, they were like a tree cut down, with no more
roots. No more life, no more fruit (Jeremiah 8:13).

But God made them a promise: "Out of the stump of David's family will grow a shoot—yes, a new Branch bearing fruit from the old root. And the Spirit of the Lord will rest on him—the Spirit of wisdom and understanding" (Isaiah 11:1–2a NLT).

One day God would send someone—someone wise—to bring his people back to life. Do you see the little shoot, coming out of the stump? That's the start. Not a huge tree, not a mighty trunk. Just a sprig. But watch what happens next.

Questions

If you were coming to save the world, how would you make your entrance? Why?

Why do you think Isaiah says that Jesus will come as a "shoot," a tiny plant?

Jesus Brings New Life

Jesus grew in wisdom and in stature and in favor with God and all the people. Luke 2:52 NLT

Do you see the little baby?

Not very big. Not very strong. Just an infant. But from this little life, more life would grow.

Do you see the little boy?

He's not grown up. But the Bible says that "Jesus grew in wisdom and in stature and in favor with God and all the people" (Luke 2:52 NLT).

When he was all grown up, no one was wiser than Jesus. And no one did more amazing things.

Like a new tree growing from the stump, Jesus was full of life and fruit. He always obeyed his Father. He always loved God. He always trusted the Lord.

And this life would branch out and spread to others. One day, Jesus told his followers: "Yes, I am the vine; you are the branches. Those who remain in me, and I in them, will produce much fruit. For apart from me you can do nothing" (John 15:5 NLT).

So, wherever Jesus went, he brought lots of life.

Jesus brought life to a little girl who had died. It wasn't even hard for him. It was like waking her from a nap. "Holding her hand, he said to her . . . 'Little girl, get up!' And the girl, who was twelve years old, immediately stood up and walked around!" (Mark 5:41–42a NLT).

Jesus brought life to other people as well. He brought life to hands that couldn't work anymore. He brought life to legs that couldn't run anymore. He brought life to hearts that didn't love anymore.

He was the source of life. He is the source of your life. He is the true and fruitful Branch.

Questions

What parts of your life do you get from Jesus? (This may be a trick question.)

How might this change the way you think about praying to the Lord?

Day 3: A Promise to Remember

Jesus Gives Us Strength

Don't be afraid, for I am with you. Don't be discouraged, for I am your God. I will strengthen you and help you. I will hold you up with my victorious right hand. Isaiah 41:10 NLT

Have you ever opened a present for Christmas or a birthday only to discover that you couldn't play with it right away? Maybe it needed to be removed from lots of plastic and packaging. Or maybe it came in parts that needed to be put together. And this is where mom or dad, or grandpa or grandma, are so wonderful.

They always seem to know what to do. They know how to help you. And they want to help you. So you know that whatever gift you might get this Christmas—even a toy that you can't figure out on your own—they'll be there to help you.

And that's what the Promise to Remember verse says as well. You'll find help—not with difficult presents, but with the hard things in life. And not about getting help from someone in your family, but about the help that comes from the Lord himself. He promises, "I will strengthen you, I will help you" (Isaiah 41:10b).

The Lord Jesus is the source of your life; he is the true vine (John 15:1), the true and fruitful branch. And no matter what you face tomorrow or the next day or the next, he has everything you will need. He will help you, and you will get your strength from him. So no matter what happens, you don't need to be afraid. The Lord will give you strength. He's got you, and he will calm your fears.

Questions

Last week, what did you need help with?

Last year, what do you remember needing help with?

How can you look to Jesus to strengthen and help you this week?

Day 4: A Challenge to Accept

We Can Trust the Lord

Trust in the LORD always, for the LORD GOD is the eternal Rock. Isaiah 26:4 NLT

When your family gets together—to watch something or pray together or just hang out—where's your favorite place to sit? Isn't it great to have a nice spot where you can sit, pull up a blanket or soft pillow, and just enjoy time together as a family?

But imagine what would happen if the couch cushion you're sitting on, just fell through? And you found yourself stuck down in the couch? Or if the back of your chair gave way, and you had to catch yourself from falling backward. That'd be crazy and a bit scary, right? Why? Because when you sit down, you expect the couch or the chair to be there for you—not to cave in or collapse.

That is a great picture of what the Bible calls trust. Today's verse says "Trust in the Lord always." Why? Because God is an "eternal Rock." If you thought the couch or chair was going to fall apart, you'd never sit on it, right? This verse challenges us to put our full weight on the Lord. You can trust him. Whatever hard time you might be having, whatever is just no fun, you can go to the Lord and tell him about it.

Every day for the rest of your life, the Lord can be the favorite place you love to be. He will never move. You can trust him. You can put your full weight on him, always.

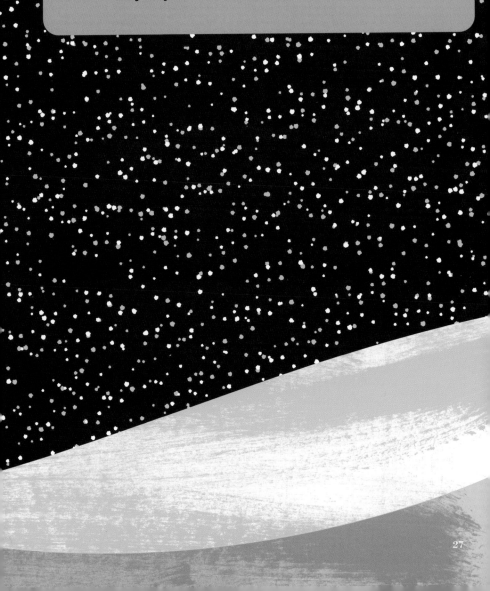

Questions

What's something that's easy to trust the Lord about?

What's something that's harder to trust the Lord about?

Why do you think there's a difference?

Day 5: Family Fun

When Jesus came to earth, he told us how much we needed him—like tree branches need to be connected to the tree and its roots. Read these words of Jesus and think about how much we all need Jesus and his strength every day:

"I am the true grapevine, and my Father is the gardener. . . . Remain in me, and I will remain in you. For a branch cannot produce fruit if it is severed from the vine, and you cannot be fruitful unless you remain in me. Yes, I am the vine; you are the branches. Those who remain in me, and I in them, will produce much fruit. For apart from me you can do nothing." John 15:1, 4–5 NLT

After this Christmas carol, you'll find lots of fun for the whole family: crafts and other activities.

Come, Thou Long-Expected Jesus

Come, thou long-expected Jesus,
Born to set thy people free;
From our fears and sins release us,
Let us find our rest in thee.
Israel's strength and consolation,
Hope of all the earth thou art;
Dear Desire of every nation,
Joy of every longing heart.

Joy to those who long to see thee,
Dayspring from on high, appear;
Come, thou promised Rod of Jesse,
Of thy birth we long to hear!
O'er the hills the angels singing
News, glad tidings of a birth;
"Go to him, your praises bringing;
Christ the Lord has come to earth."

Come to earth to taste our sadness,
He whose glories knew no end;
By his life he brings us gladness,
Our Redeemer, Shepherd, Friend.
Leaving riches without number,
Born within a cattle stall;
This the everlasting wonder,
Christ was born the Lord of all.

Born thy people to deliver,
Born a child and yet a king,
Born to reign in us forever,
Now thy gracious kingdom bring.
By thine own eternal Spirit
Rule in all our hearts alone;
By thine all-sufficient merit,
Raise us to thy glorious throne.

Charles Wesley

Craft

Week 2: Ornament

Supplies You'll Need: Week 2 ornament craft (one copy for each child); coloring/art supplies; scissors; glue stick or tape; yarn or string. Note: Scan the QR code at the back of the book to access digital copies of the ornament crafts.

Directions: Cut out the ornament copy and have the children decorate the design. Read the "Isaiah says" and the "Jesus says" statements. Then have the children write their answer to the "I say" statement. Fold the ornament on the dotted line. Make a string or yarn loop for hanging and tuck it into the fold. Tape or glue the ornament closed.

Ornament Questions

What does Isaiah say?
Answer: "A shoot will grow."

What does Jesus say?
Answer: "I am the true vine."

What do we say and believe?
Answer: "Jesus gives me life."

Jesus says: "I am the true vine." Jn 15:1

Isaiah says: "A shoot will grow." Is 11:1

I SAY:

Other Activities

Activity #1

Supplies You'll Need: dried beans, disposable cups, potting soil, pen

Grow Your Own Plant

Take some dried beans (lima beans or kidney beans) and soak them overnight. Then plant a few in a disposable cup filled with plain potting soil. Also be sure to poke some holes in the bottom of the cup to allow excess water to drain away. Each child can write their name on the cup and water the growing seeds each day.

You can spend time talking about what seeds need to grow, and what we need to do in order to grow.

You may also want to remind your children that when Jesus came, he wasn't big and strong like a tree. Isaiah says he was like a "young plant, and like a root out of dry ground" (Isaiah 53:2). He was weak and little—a tiny baby—just like the tiny shoots growing in the cups.

Activity #2

Help Serve Others

Together with your children think of someone you can help (just like Jesus helps us). Perhaps you can make some cookies together and deliver them as a family. Or you could arrange a time to call or video chat with someone who might be lonely. What can you do together to help and encourage someone else?

Activity #3
Supplies You'll Need: roll of plastic wrap, candy or small prizes, timer, socks (one pair)

Unroll the Fun

Play this game as a follow-up to the Promise to Remember. To prepare, take a roll of plastic wrap, and without cutting it begin to wrap pieces of candy or small surprises/toys into the plastic wrap, tightly turning it over and over into the shape of a ball.

Gather everyone into a circle. Starting with the youngest person, have them slip the socks onto their hands. Set the timer for one minute, and have them try to unwrap the plastic ball. (They get to keep whatever candy/prizes they unwrap.) When time is up, the ball goes to the next youngest person, etc. The rotation continues until the ball of plastic wrap is completely unwrapped.

Activity #4
Supplies You'll Need: paper, pen or pencil

Paint Your Place

Have each child draw a picture of their favorite spot to sit (either with the family or when alone). Ask them to draw what makes it so special to them.

Remind them how Jesus is the Rock we can trust and put our full weight upon.

Week Three

The Third Wonder

Jesus Is the Good Shepherd
and He Carries Us Close

Jesus Leads Us Gently

He will feed his flock like a shepherd. He will carry the lambs in his arms, holding them close to his heart. He will gently lead the mother sheep with their young. Isaiah 40:11 NLT

When someone comes back from the store with food for a Christmas party, isn't it fun to help carry in the bags full of Christmas snacks and surprises!

If you're a good helper, do you carry everything the same way?

What if you set down the eggs like you'd throw down the paper towels? What if you held a bunch of tomatoes just like you would a bag of potatoes? What if you grabbed the bread like a can of soup?

There might be a mess and another trip to the store.

But think for a moment, how you would hold a baby. Not like potatoes, not like tomatoes. And not like bread or eggs. As a good helper, you'd be careful and gentle. Soft but strong. Why?

Because little babies can't protect themselves. And they aren't strong enough to hold on for themselves. So when they need to be carried, you pick them up. And when they're crying, you hold them securely. And even when they're heavy, you just don't quit.

Did you know that this is how the Lord treats his people? In the Bible, we read how God's people decided not to obey God anymore. The Bible describes them as sheep wandering away from their shepherd.

Even when his people wandered, the Lord promised that he would still take care of them: "He will feed his flock like a shepherd. He will carry the lambs in his arms, holding them close to his heart. He will gently lead the mother sheep with their young" (Isaiah 40:11 NLT).

Questions

Have you ever wandered away from the Lord—doing your own thing?

How do you think the Lord thought about you when you wandered from him?

Day 2: A Closer Look

Jesus Knows How to Help You

"I am the good shepherd; I know my own sheep, and they know me." John 10:14 NLT

Like a shepherd, God loves to help his people, even the ones who have wandered away from him. But he doesn't help everyone in the same way.

In a flock, the little lambs weren't strong enough to keep up with the rest of the sheep. They needed to be carried. So the shepherd would pick them up—not with a sigh, but with a smile. A weight on his shoulders but never a burden. Because the shepherd would hold them not just in his arms, he would hold them in his heart.

Some mother sheep were ready to have baby lambs. Carrying the extra weight made them tired. Their legs hurt. Their backs hurt. They were worn out. And they couldn't keep up with the others.

But the shepherd would know all this. And he would lead them gently, taking it slow and easy. This is the kind of shepherd that God had promised would come.

And one day, Jesus came. He was the true Shepherd of his people. And he was gentle—even in his heart. He said, "I am the good shepherd; I know my own sheep, and they know me" (John 10:14 NLT).

So whatever your name, whatever you're like—he knows you. And he knows how to help you.

Whether you're young or old, strong or weak; whether you're good or bad, or happy or sad; whatever burdens you're carrying, Jesus, the Shepherd, is good. And he will carry you.

Questions

What does it mean that Jesus will carry you?

When might that make you glad, and when might that not be what you'd want?

Day 3: A Promise to Remember

Jesus Helps the Weak

He gives power to the weak and strength to the powerless. Isaiah 40:29 NLT

What if I promised that when you're grumpy, you can have a piece of candy? Or that if your room is messy, you can watch your favorite show? That doesn't seem to make a lot of sense does it? Why do good things for people when they haven't done their part, right?

But did you know this makes sense to Jesus?

Our verse today says this: If you are so tired that you can't take another step, Jesus will help you. Now if we were writing this verse, we might say: If you have tried really hard and you didn't give up, then Jesus will see your effort and help you. But this verse actually says, if you have no effort to give, Jesus will help you (Matthew 11:28).

So always remember that you don't have to get things all figured out to ask Jesus for help. You don't have to be strong to ask for his strength. You don't have to try your best so he will help you.

All you need to do is tell him how weak you are, how worn out you are, how much you need him. And he will hear you, he will help you, and he will give you strength.

Questions

How do you feel about people when they don't seem strong or good or smart enough?

Why is it hard to treat other people like today's verse says Jesus treats you when you're weak?

Day 4: A Challenge to Accept

Wait for the Lord

But they who wait for the LORD shall renew their strength; they shall mount up with wings like eagles; they shall run and not be weary; they shall walk and not faint. Isaiah 40:31

How many days are there until Christmas? Do you know? Are you waiting and counting the days?

It's exciting to wait for something that's going to be amazing! Perhaps you've not been really waiting, but have even sneaked into the room where the presents are and tried to do a little guesswork—shaking boxes and trying to imagine what's on the inside.

The Challenge to Accept for this week is to think about the Lord, like you're already thinking about your presents.

The verse says we are to "wait for the Lord." That doesn't mean that he's busy and we're going to have to wait our turn for him to help us. But it does mean that sometimes he doesn't help as soon as we would like.

Sometimes we want the Lord to help us right now—like we are in charge and he's not obeying us. But the Lord knows the best way to help us and the best time to help us. So sometimes this means we have to wait for his very good plan. And you might be tempted to try to speed things up—to stop waiting for him.

But sometimes the Lord wants you to just trust him, to put your hope in him. To just wait for his timing (Psalm 39:7).

Questions

Why is it so hard to wait?

Why is it hard to wait for the Lord's way? Or for his timing?

Day 5: Family Fun

When Jesus came, he told everyone that he was the Shepherd that Isaiah had written about. He would take care of all God's people—feeding them, loving them, and protecting them—even if it cost his own life. And it would.

"I am the good shepherd; I know my own sheep, and they know me, just as my Father knows me and I know the Father. So I sacrifice my life for the sheep." John 10:14–15 NLT

After this Christmas carol, you'll find lots of fun for the whole family: crafts and other activities.

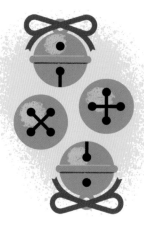

Joy to the World

Joy to the world! the Lord is come;
Let earth receive her King;
Let every heart prepare him room,
And heaven and nature sing,
And heaven and nature sing,
And heaven, and heaven, and nature sing.

Joy to the world! the Savior reigns;
Let men their songs employ;
While fields and floods, rocks, hills, and plains
Repeat the sounding joy,
Repeat the sounding joy,
Repeat, repeat the sounding joy.

No more let sins and sorrows grow,
Nor thorns infest the ground;
He comes to make his blessings flow
Far as the curse is found,
Far as the curse is found,
Far as, far as, the curse is found.

He rules the world with truth and grace,
And makes the nations prove
The glories of his righteousness,
And wonders of his love,
And wonders of his love,
And wonders, wonders, of his love.

Isaac Watts

Craft

Week 3: Ornament

Supplies You'll Need: Week 3 ornament craft (one copy for each child); coloring/art supplies; scissors; glue stick or tape; yarn or string. Note: Scan the QR code at the back of the book to access digital copies of the ornament crafts.

Directions: Cut out the ornament copy and have the children decorate the design. Read the "Isaiah says" and the "Jesus says" statements. Then have the children write their answer to the "I say" statement. Fold the ornament on the dotted line. Make a string or yarn loop for hanging and tuck it into the fold. Tape or glue the ornament closed.

Ornament Questions

What does Isaiah say?
Answer: "He will carry the lambs in his arms."

What does Jesus say?
Answer: "I am the good Shepherd."

What do we say and believe?
Answer: "Jesus carries me close."

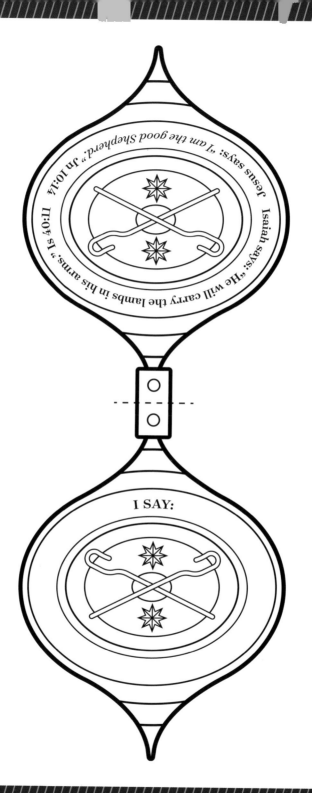

Jesus says: "I am the good Shepherd." Jn 10:14

Isaiah says: "He will carry the lambs in his arms." Is 40:11

I SAY:

Other Activities

Activity #1

The Art of Encouragement

Jesus knows how to take care of each of his sheep. He knows which ones are sad, which ones are tired, which ones are having a hard time. So have each child think of someone you know—perhaps a neighbor, family member, or someone at church—who might also need some encouragement.

Once each child has selected a different name, ask him/her to think of what kind of craft or drawing might be most encouraging or helpful to that person. Then once the projects are done, you can deliver these personalized art projects together, praying for each person and explaining how each project was meant just for them.

Activity #2:

Supplies You'll Need: empty toilet paper roll (one for each person), cotton balls, glue

Make Woolly, Woolly Fun Decorations

Make Christmas decorations that look like sheep. You can use a toilet paper roll and cotton balls, with some glue. Before starting decide what kind of sheep to make. Pick a name and an attitude: happy, sad, weak, strong, etc. Hang these different sheep on your tree, or add them to a crèche/nativity scene.

Activity #3:

Supplies You'll Need: various household objects; wrapping paper; tape

Guess the Gift

Wrap five common household objects as Christmas presents.
Then have the children try to guess what each one is, just
by holding and shaking it. See which child can get the most
correct guesses.

Activity #4:

Supplies You'll Need: various food items; blindfold

Name That Food

To prepare for this guessing game, select 8–10 different small
food items (for example, an egg, a slice of bread, a tomato, a
potato, a carrot, a celery stalk, a can of soup, etc.). Then
blindfold a child and have them try to identify a few of the items,
using only their feet (or nose). Can they tell what each item
is? If other children are watching, you will want to introduce
different items for each child's turn.

Point out that there's no guessing with the Lord. He knows what
each of us is like and how to take care of us.

Christmas Punch

Did you know that Saint Nick was a real person who lived about 1700 years ago? In fact, good old Saint Nick was a pastor, named Nicholas, who lived in the city of Myra. (Myra is near the modern town of Demre, located in the nation of Turkey.)

Pastor Nicholas loved Jesus, and he loved God's Word. And one year (about 325 years after Jesus was born), Nicholas traveled over 400 miles north to the city of Nicea. Nicholas was going to a pastor's meeting in that city. Over 300 pastors would meet together and talk about the Bible. They wanted to discuss and learn more of what the Bible taught about Jesus.

Another pastor at the meeting was named Arius. Now Arius said that he believed the Bible but then he said he did not believe that Jesus was God. Arius said that Jesus was a really important human being—but not God. This was wrong, and Nicholas knew it!

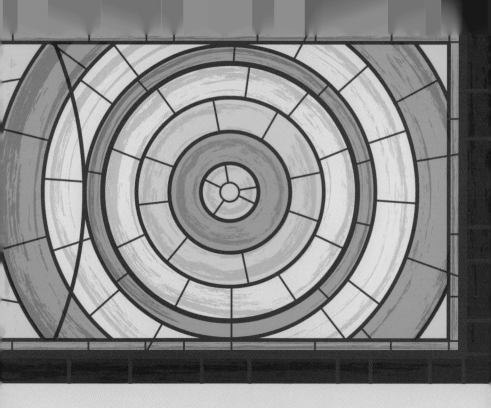

During the meeting, as Arius was telling everyone that Jesus was not God, Pastor Nicholas became really upset. This was NOT what the Bible taught. So, maybe trying to knock some sense into Arius, Pastor Nicholas made the first Christmas punch! Really! He shouldn't have, but he became so upset that he actually punched Arius.

If you've been bad this year, Saint Nick might put coal in your stocking. But if you teach bad things about Jesus, you might want to duck.[2]

Week Four

The Fourth Wonder

Jesus Is God with Us
and He Calms Our Fear

Day 1: Picture It

God Will Be with You

When you pass through the waters, I will be with you; and through the rivers, they shall not overwhelm you; when you walk through fire you shall not be burned, and the flame shall not consume you. Isaiah 43:2

December 25 is about a week away, and everything is almost ready for Christmas. Perhaps you've been enjoying Christmas lights. Or maybe you've been singing Christmas songs—songs about bells jingling all the way, about going "over the river and through the woods," or about "chestnuts roasting on an open fire."

What holiday fun! Sledding over wintry rivers and standing before a crackling fire.

But wait a minute. Rivers and fires? Is it really all that fun?

Today's verse talks about deep water. And when someone is learning to swim for the first time, a river can be scary. Just getting close to the deep end of the pool can fill a heart with fear.

But, what if someone who could swim, someone who could help you, was with you? Right beside you. Now how would you feel?

Today's verse also talks about fire. And when someone comes inside from the cold and sees a cheerful fire in the fireplace, getting close can seem warm and inviting. But if you get too close to a flame, even a tiny candle is too hot.

But, what if you were protected? What if, like in the story of Shadrach, Meshach, and Abednego (see Daniel 3), someone was with you—someone who would guard you even from the fire?

Water and fire. They can seem simple and even the stuff we sing about at Christmas.

But they can be scary too. Deep waters. Dangerous fire. Yet even then, God has promised always to be at your side.

He said, "When you pass through the waters, I will be with you; and through the rivers, they shall not overwhelm you; when you walk through fire you shall not be burned, and the flame shall not consume you" (Isaiah 43:2).

Questions

Can you think of situations that make you afraid?

How is Jesus near you at those times?

Day 2: A Closer Look

He Is Near; You Need Not Fear

"Behold, the virgin shall conceive and bear a son, and they shall call his name Immanuel" (which means, God with us). Matthew 1:23 (compare with Isaiah 7:14)

As you grow up, you may not face surging waters. You may not feel actual raging fires.

But life can be difficult. And it's easy to be scared.

You might wonder, "What will happen tomorrow? What am I going to do? Who will be with me?"

The Lord had promised his people that whatever happened—no matter how afraid they were—he would never leave them (Deuteronomy 31:6). He would come be with them. And that's exactly what he did.

One day a baby would be born, and they would "call his name Immanuel (which means God with us)" (Matthew 1:23). And as promised, he would be with his people through surging waters and raging fire.

So after Jesus calms a storm on the sea, he asks the disciples, "Why are you afraid?" (Matthew 8:26).

And when the fires of God's anger burned against our sin, he took our sins—and the punishment we deserve—on himself (Isaiah 53:5).

So that even when Jesus was returning to the Father, he could say, "I am with you always, to the end of the age" (Matthew 28:20).

Remember: no matter what you face that makes you fear, the Lord has promised: "I am near."

Questions

When you were little, what used to help you not be afraid? Why?

What about Jesus's being near can help you not be afraid?

Day 3: A Promise to Remember

God Is Our Shelter and Shade

For you have been a stronghold to the poor, a stronghold to the needy in his distress, a shelter from the storm and a shade from the heat. Isaiah 25:4a

Which do you like better: hot weather or cold weather? If you don't like the cold, you probably go outside with your coat zipped up or like to stay inside wrapped in a blanket. Or if you don't like the heat, then on hot sunny days, you might wear a hat or stay in the shade.

But whether you like it warmer or cooler, what helps is to stay close to what keeps you warm or keeps you cool. If you like it warm, you stay close to coats or blankets. If you like it cool, you stay close to whatever might give you some shade.

That's what the verse today promises: the Lord is a stronghold (or refuge), a shelter and a shade from the heat.

He protects and helps by staying close to us. He is with us, always, wherever we are and wherever we go. And that's how we can enjoy his protection (Psalm 121:4–6). He keeps us safe, because he is with us.

Questions

How can you get close to the Lord and his protection?

How can you stay close to the Lord and his protection?

Day 4: A Challenge to Accept

Look Only to God

Turn to me and be saved, all the ends of the earth!
For I am God, and there is no other. Isaiah 45:22

Give me your best answer. Question 1: What is your favorite day in December for Christmas? Question 2: Which nose do you like best—your left one or your right one?

Of course, there's only one day that's Christmas—December 25. And you only have one nose, not two. Today's verse is trying to get us to see the same kind of thing is true about God.

There's only one God. And there is nothing else that is God besides him.

Sometimes people think they can find help from something other than God—so they rely on themselves, they follow their heart, or they count on money or other people to save the day. But there is only one God. Only one Rescuer—only one Savior (Isaiah 43:11).

Anything or anyone else is not really a rescuer at all. When it comes to who can truly help and save the day—there's only One.

Jesus came to rescue us, to help us. And our challenge is to turn to him when we need help. To look to him as our Savior, not to anyone or anything else.

Questions

What kind of things does Jesus save from?

What kind of hard things do you need rescuing from?

Star of Wonder

[The wise men asked,] "Where is he who has been born king of the Jews? For we saw his star when it rose and have come to worship him." Matthew 2:2

For almost 2,000 years people have wondered what exactly was the star that led the wise men to Bethlehem. Was it a brand new star that just appeared one night? But how could a star actually lead people?

More than that, how could a star identify one particular house among many others in the village of Bethlehem? (Think about it—would you ever give directions to where you live by explaining that you—but not your neighbor—lived beneath a particular star?)

In 2015 Colin Nicholl, a Bible scholar, working with astronomers, made a simply stellar discovery—which fits both the Bible and astronomy. Nicholl says that the Star of Bethlehem was most likely a comet (which were commonly called "stars" back then—like we still call meteors "shooting stars" today).

If you'd like to learn more, you can read about it online or in Colin Nicholl's book, *The Great Christ Comet*.[3]

Day 5: Family Fun

Jesus is Immanuel, which means God with us (Matthew 1:23). The apostle John said the same thing about Jesus:

And the Word became flesh and dwelt among us, and we have seen his glory, glory as of the only Son from the Father, full of grace and truth. John 1:14

In Jesus Christ, God has come near to us and has promised that he will always be with us. Before he returned to heaven, Jesus said: "Go therefore and make disciples of all nations, baptizing them in the name of the Father and of the Son and of the Holy Spirit, teaching them to observe all that I have commanded you. And behold, I am with you always, to the end of the age" (Matthew 28:19–20).

After this Christmas carol, you'll find lots of fun for the whole family: crafts and other activities.

O Come, O Come, Emmanuel

O come, O come, Emmanuel,
And ransom captive Israel,
That mourns in lonely exile here
Until the Son of God appear.
Rejoice! Rejoice! Emmanuel
Shall come to thee, O Israel.

O come, Thou Rod of Jesse, free
Thine own from Satan's tyranny;
From depths of hell thy people save,
And give them victory o'er the grave.
Rejoice! Rejoice! Emmanuel
Shall come to thee, O Israel.

O come, Thou Dayspring, from on high,
And cheer us by thy drawing nigh;
Disperse the gloomy clouds of night,
And death's dark shadows put to flight.
Rejoice! Rejoice! Emmanuel
Shall come to thee, O Israel.

Craft

Week 4: Ornament

Supplies You'll Need: Week 4 ornament craft (one copy for each child); coloring/art supplies; scissors; glue stick or tape; yarn or string. Note: Scan the QR code at the back of the book to access digital copies of the ornament crafts.

Directions: Cut out the ornament copy and have the children decorate the design. Read the "Isaiah says" and the "Jesus says" statements. Then have the children write their answer to the "I say" statement. Fold the ornament on the dotted line. Make a string or yarn loop for hanging and tuck it into the fold. Tape or glue the ornament closed.

Ornament Questions

What does Isaiah say?
Answer: "I will be with you."

What does Jesus say?
Answer: "I am with you always."

What do we say and believe?
Answer: "Jesus calms my fears."

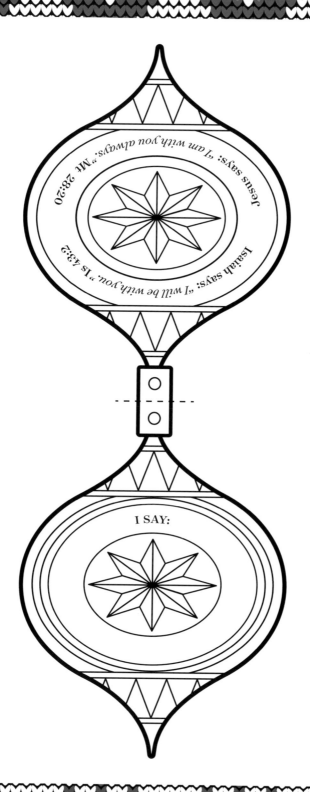

Jesus says: "I am with you always." Mt. 28:20

Isaiah says: "I will be with you." Is 43:2

I SAY:

Other Activities

Activity #1:
Supplies You'll Need: some coins (5 per child); tape or string

Christmas Coin Toss

How close can you get? Give each child five coins, and have them stand the same distance from a wall (about 5-6 feet). You could also mark a line on the floor with a string or some tape.

Then have each child toss a coin toward the wall. The object is to see who can get closest to the wall without touching it. If a coin hits the wall, it doesn't count. The child with the closest coin is the winner, or the child with the most coins closest to the wall is the winner. This game can be a reminder that Jesus is always close to us.

Activity #2:
Supplies You'll Need: various Christmas-themed objects

Hotter/Colder Scavenger Hunt

You're getting closer. Select some object around your house that's somehow related to Christmas. Hide that object somewhere around the house and have your children search for it. You can give them clues about how "hot" or "cold" they are—i.e., whether they're getting nearer or farther away from the hidden object.

The goal is to get close and find the object. We may find it difficult to find the object, but the Lord is always near us.

Activity #3:

Supplies You'll Need: various (perhaps cardboard; tape; paper; and cotton balls; etc.) and some eggs

Egg-breaking Egg-stravaganza

Give each child the same craft items of your choice—perhaps some cardboard, tape, paper, and cotton balls. Then have each one design a protective container to hold a single egg. They can also decorate their containers with Christmas colors and designs.

Once the containers are finished and the egg is placed inside each one. Drop the container (with the egg inside) from counter-height onto the kitchen floor. (It might get messy.)

The object is to see which container provides the best protection to the egg inside. You might also want to video each egg drop using the slow-motion feature on your smart phone.

How does this activity provide comparisons—or more likely, contrasts—with the protection that Jesus provides?

Activity #4:

Making Time

Just like the Lord is always near us, is there someone that you and your children can visit and be near? Brainstorm with your children to come up with someone else you can take time to just be with sometime this week.

Christmas Day

The Fifth Wonder

Jesus Is the Bread of Life
and He Feeds Us Freely

Come to the Table

Come, everyone who thirsts, come to the waters; and he who has no money, come, buy and eat! Come, buy wine and milk without money and without price.
Isaiah 55:1

What is your favorite thing to eat at Christmas dinner?

Is it the rolls or mac and cheese? Do you prefer turkey or ham? Or would you just rather have pizza? And what about for dessert?

Over the last few weeks, we've been learning about Jesus. Like sitting at a four-course meal, we've had the wonders of his love spread before us.

In our darkness, he opens our eyes. He's the light who makes us see (Isaiah 9:2; John 8:12).

We have no real life without him. He's the fruitful branch—the vine—who gives us life (Isaiah 11:1–2a; John 15:1, 4–5).

When we have no more strength, he helps us. He's the Good Shepherd who carries us close (Isaiah 40:11; John 10:14).

And when we're scared, he keeps us safe. He will never, ever leave us. He is Immanuel, God with us (Isaiah 43:2; Matthew 1:23; 28:20).

But does all this seem too good to be true? After all, maybe he can make blind eyes see, but why would he open mine?

He's the source of all I really need, the fruitful branch and the vine. But do I really deserve the life he gives?

What if I have no more strength—because I've not been good and done my best?

And how do I know that one day I won't do something that'll finally make him give up on me? Isn't this a four-course banquet that's just too good to be true?

The answer is yes—and no.

Yes, it is too good to be true—if you're paying for this four-course meal. You'll never be good enough. You'll never be strong enough. You'll never be brave enough to earn a spot at the table.

So yes, you don't have enough to make him love you like this (Romans 3:23–24).

But the answer is also No. It's not too good to be true. In fact, it's because it's so good that it is true.

Long ago, the Lord said, "Come, everyone who thirsts, come to the waters; and he who has no money, come, buy and eat! Come, buy wine and milk without money and without price" (Isaiah 55:1).

The Lord invites you to his feast. But before you can sit and eat, he requires something from you.

If you checked your pockets to see if you had enough money to enjoy the feast of God's love, how much would be enough? He asks you to bring one thing—empty pockets. All you need is your need.

Are you hungry for the Lord? Do you thirst for his love? Then you have all that you need. Nothing further is due. So pull up a chair. The banquet is ready. Your place has been set.

But how is all of this free?

Jesus said, "I am the living bread that came down from heaven. If anyone eats of this bread, he will live forever. And the bread that I will give for the life of the world is my flesh" (John 6:51).

Jesus is the bread of life. He paid the price (1 Peter 1:18–19). He gave his life to give you life. He purchased your place at the table.

He was forsaken by the Father on the cross, so you could be welcomed to the feast forever (Revelation 22:17).

Because of Jesus, we can enjoy the

Wonders of His Love

Questions

What kinds of things can you do to make Jesus like you more? (This might be another trick question.)

What makes the freeness of the Lord's invitation such amazing news (reread today's verse)?

X-Mas?

Have you ever seen a sign that says Xmas instead of Christmas?
Do you know what that means?

Some people don't like seeing Xmas signs. Because they think that
the sign is part of a secret plan to "take Christ out of Christmas."
And that's kind of true—the letters C-H-R-I-S-T are missing. But did
you know that while Xmas isn't part of a secret plan, it does contain
a secret code?

In the Greek alphabet, like in English, the third from the last letter
is X. In English we call this letter EX. But in Greek, X is the letter
chi, pronounced KHEE. This letter is the first letter in the Greek
name Christ. It's spelled this way: X (the letter chi), R (the letter rho,
which looks like the letter p, pronounced ROE), I (the letter iota,
pronounced YO-tah), S (the letter sigma, pronounced as it looks),
T (tau, pronounced TAUW, as in "cow").

So, the reason that some people spell Christmas as Xmas is because
X—the first letter in the Greek spelling of Christ—is an abbreviation
of the name Christ. Just like you might say LOL (for "laugh out loud")
or ask for your favorite multi-colored M&Ms (which stands for Mars
& Murrie's—bet you didn't know that!), the X in Xmas stands for the
whole name of Christ.

Can you match the Greek letters to their English equivalents?
(It might take some careful thinking, and re-reading the information
above, too.)

Greek	English
τ	Ch
X	r
σ	i
ι	s
ρ	t

Now take a moment and practice writing out the entire name of
Christ using only Greek letters.[4]

Hark! the Herald Angels Sing

Hark! the herald angels sing,
"Glory to the newborn King,
Peace on earth, and mercy mild,
God and sinners reconciled!"
Joyful, all ye nations rise,
Join the triumph of the skies;
With th' angelic host proclaim,
"Christ is born in Bethlehem!"
Hark! the herald angels sing,
"Glory to the newborn King!"

Christ, by highest heaven adored;
Christ, the everlasting Lord;
Late in time behold him come,
Offspring of the Virgin's womb.
Veiled in flesh the Godhead see;
Hail th' incarnate Deity,
Pleased as man with man to dwell,
Jesus, our Emmanuel.
Hark! the herald angels sing,
"Glory to the newborn King!"

Hail the heav'n-born Prince of Peace!
Hail the Sun of Righteousness!
Light and life to all he brings,
Ris'n with healing in his wings.
Mild he lays his glory by,
Born that man no more may die,
Born to raise the sons of earth,
Born to give us second birth.
Hark! the herald angels sing,
"Glory to the newborn King!"

Charles Wesley

Scan this QR code to access digital
copies of the ornament crafts.

---

[1]Kenneth E. Bailey, *Jesus Through Middle Eastern Eyes*, (Downers
Grove, IL: InterVarsity Press, 2008), 25–37.

[2]Thanks to Michael Reeves for this wordplay on "Christmas
punch." Michael Reeves, *Rejoicing in Christ*, (Downers Grove, IL:
IVP Academic, 2015), 19.

[3]Champ Thornton, *The Radical Book for Kids*, (Greensboro, NC:
New Growth, 2016), 141.

[4]For more on the Greek alphabet and fun you can have with it,
see *The Radical Book for Kids*, pages 199–201.

New Growth Press, Greensboro, NC 27401
Text Copyright © 2021 by George Thomas Thornton II
Illustration Copyright © 2021 by New Growth Press

Cover/Interior Design/Illustrations: Jeremy Slagle, slagledesign.com

ISBN: 978-1-64507-157-0
Library of Congress Control Number: 2021015840

Printed in India

29 28 27 26 25 24 23 22   2 3 4 5 6